Having Said That

Jack Roberts

©2014 AMERICANA eBooks, Szeged

Jack Roberts: *Having Said That*

ISBN: 978-615-5423-04-8

AMERICANA eBooks is a division of *AMERICANA – E-Journal of American Studies in Hungary*, published by the Department of American Studies, University of Szeged, Hungary.
ebooks.americanaejournal.hu

Cover image by György Novák
Book design by Zoltán Dragon

Having Said That

Jack Roberts

CONTENTS

Re: Bright Goddess, At Your Rising

> If business is not properly run the rites and music will not be honored if the rites and music be not honored, penalties and punishments will not achieve the intended effects of equity and justice. The people won't know where to place their feet... or to whom they should stretch out their hands.
> — *Digest of the Analects*

...sure you'll do your utmost to make our visitor feel welcome. Huang has been—

The voicemail heralding the arrival of another consultant from corporate had just expressed every confidence in my aptitude for displaying goodwill toward strangers when a dark young man wearing a red silk jacket in the old Chinese style appeared at my cubicle.

I missed his first quiet words to me since he had begun to speak before I could restore the headset to its cradle and turn to face him: "—sent to help this branch make a smooth transition to the new calendar." How weird would that have been: the stranger from corporate delivering the rest of the message I'd interrupted, that message resuming and concluding in the mouth of one whose arrival at branch was its subject? It was too early in the day, too early in the work week for crazy shit like that to start happening. But the stranger spoke in a soft, reedy voice that I had to strain to understand, so perhaps I hadn't heard him right.

A delicate hand hovered before me… let's say that a hand drifted toward me in a manner suggesting particular refinement then paused and waited as its owner waited for a faint smile to pass across his lips before he said, "I am Huang."

"Ken LeBrun," I said, clasping his hand, gauging my grasp for fear of squeezing too hard. I needn't have worried: Huang's grip was strong and firm.

"The Bear. Very good. I look forward to working with you, Ken the Bear."

"Likewise." I tried to smile but something was wrong here. He seemed to lace his speech with foreign cadences and verbal patterns aimed at creating the impression that English was not his first language. This way of talking and that firm handshake had me questioning my first impression of Huang.

His oriental get-up, his serene, even mystical bearing, his delicacy of manner and gesture: these had fostered my initial sense of Huang as a small Chinese man finely framed. But Huang wasn't who he seemed to be, or, if most of him was, some of him was not. Nor would that some ever be if it had its way. Though I gave him all the credit in the world for going to the lengths he'd gone to cultivate a nearly perfect illusion, I wasn't buying the Asian act.

I took a step back to get a better look at him. He'd seemed so much smaller up close; he'd made himself look shorter up close. What's more, he'd achieved this effect in full knowledge and with strong intention. I took another step back. Gone was the profound difference in our heights. I had two three inches on him. At most. A few more minutes and I'd have begun to this too. No, Huang was of more than average height with a wiry build. Closer inspection of Huang's face and hair would yield this account: all black curls and eyes. To compare him to someone almost famous: he looked like Sal Bando, mustachioed captain and third baseman (lifetime batting average: .254; 242 HR) of the Oakland A's during their championship years (1972, 1973, 1974), though lacked the major-league facial hair.

Huang turned as if to go, then turned back to face me again. "Ken the Bear, I do not wish to give offense, but may I abandon the formalities that accompany preliminary exchanges such as this one."

"Go for it, Huang."

"Very good. I have some expertise in the care of the soul. I may possess the cure you seek."

"My soul is sick?"

Huang nodded. From his sleeve he produced a circular two-sided mirror. An inscription ran along the edge of one side: *A captive at the Palace of Vermillion Clouds, the Goddess of Disillusion made this mirror for you.* "Look upon the reverse side only," Huang said. "In a few days, your soul shall be at rest."

"Does corporate know about this?" I said, taking the mirror from Huang.

"O, yes. It is part of my brief, though a small part."

"Will you submit a report on…"

"…the health of your soul? Your condition and its cure are none of corporate's affair. I made this clear to the directors when I accepted this assignment." Huang moved on to the next cubicle. I turned the mirror over and looked into the reverse side. A gruesome skeleton stared back at me through hollow orbits. I tried to remember Huang's instructions. He had said the reverse side. I nipped the mirror over anyway. I stared into the glass and saw Phoenix, whose real name was Peggy Schnitzler, staring back at me. Looking lovelier than in life, she beckoned to me. I turned the mirror over again. The skeleton gawked. I slipped the mirror into my desk drawer and covered my face with my hands.

From that Sunday two weeks ago when I resolved to have nothing more to do with Phoenix a.k.a. Peggy, her image had attended me constantly, tested me, triggered unrelenting desire. I'd given way to bad habits and slept only poorly. You might say her image haunted me, but that verb won't capture the degree to which it simultaneously enchanted me and made me want to run. As alluring as she could be, Phoenix-Peggy never ceased to vex the hell out of me. I'd never been able to get past the pretentious name she'd given herself and all the silly affectations that went with it. All those stagy gestures she thought made her exotic and attractive: her slow-motion finger rolls calculated to show off slender digitsful of gaudy rings; her Hindu-dancer's way of making her pupils dart and jump about their sockets like waterboatmen across a pond's surface; her Lauren Bacall act: drop your chin, shoot smouldering gaze intended victim's way. I'm not saying these tricks hadn't worked their stale magic on me once, but over time they bred an eyebrow-raising if not eye-rolling distain for the magician.

The girl just tried too hard. Too often a flawed sense of occasion made her sincerest efforts at nonconformity seem forced, even ridiculous. More thought-free than freethinking, more bewildered than wild child, Phoenix-Peggy reserved a studied nakedness for the most homely of home-bound activities—writing out Christmas cards, folding laundry, watching reruns of *Family Feud.* While I never resented her nude presence in the living room—for she was lovely in and out of clothes—I had to stop myself from wincing whenever she aired out the musty cliché about how liberating it felt to be naked.

Should I add that in her spare time, Phoenix-Peggy hobbied as an artsy craftsperson, a crafty artist? She made candles, though she forgot to add the wicks sometimes.

Come Christmas, I'd mail these blue cylinders and magenta pyramids to distant relatives in distant places since, besides being wickless, grave structural flaws disqualified these forms for classroom use by teachers of solid geometry. When she remembered to add the wick, she'd fail to secure it properly in the hot liquid wax. On cooling the wick would be found worming its way free from a tiny hole near the base or coiling boa-like around the hardened mass. I'd dub these useless assemblies with names such as "Wax and String Study # 7" and make gifts of them to nice couples with whom we no longer wished to socialize.

Not a bit discouraged by her steep descent through gates of wax to candle hell, Phoenix-Peggy took up macramé. In no time, she had turned out countless wall-hangings free of those attractively repetitive patterns whose presence might otherwise have suggested the weaver's less than total commitment to undermining the foundational principles of her yarny art. Breaking new ground in the craft of folk-weaving was not without its risks. Now and then one of Phoenix-Peggy's loose-knotted designs would yield up whatever structural integrity it possessed to a passing kitty with inquiring claws. In a matter of seconds, nothing would be left of the original formlessness but a chaotic tangle of brightly-colored twine.

And Phoenix-Peggy was always on the lookout for new ways to hasten the evaporation of the last drops of my esteem for her, Just before our split, Phoenix-Peggy revealed her intention to enroll in a jewelry-making class at Waskaswaska Junior College. Visions of molten metal and scorched palms, of sharp little tools and severed digits, danced through my head. I suggested she try Japanese floral arrangement instead. "I know!" she said as if I'd made an observation. "I mean, how do they get those flowers to stay so tiny and I heard somewhat that they can even do it with cows but how can they, I mean, really?" Phoenix-Peggy snorted and left me scrambling for some shred of meaning: "What? Flowers? Tiny? Cows? Who?

You don't mean... Oh no..." Too late. All sense and coherence, like Elvis, had left the building, drained off as if someone had on the sly lowered a giant vacuum dome over our apartment complex and then waited for the signal to activate the great pump. Phoenix-Peggy's profoundly unintelligible question-statement had been the longhand signal for "Let the sucking begin." Unable to form the simplest sentence, I assumed a kneeling posture on the living room carpet. I mouthed a ritual cry. I passed an imaginary blade through my vitals. I leaned slightly to the right and toppled over into deep shag.

I probably could have put up with her anti-candles and her form-defying feats of yarn, with her irremediable misspokenness and inarticulate questions, with her silly posturing and clichéd routines. I probably could have put up with all of this for a long while had she not, late one Sunday evening, confessed to spending Saturday night in the arms of a junior vice-president for marketing. She owned up to everything not fifteen minutes after returning from Baby Pro's southwest region sales conference, an event made even more memorable for her by the launch of Baby Pro's Simulated Pregnancy Product Line. Perhaps "owned up" is not the right phrase, since I never accused her of cheating on me. If anything, I'd tried to stop her from coming clean once I figured out what she was trying to tell me. Again and again, I repeated the catch-mantra, "Hey, what happens in Tucson stays in Tucson" and added a hand gesture signifying: "Now you just go ahead and back up that rig of yours on account of we're not taking any more deliveries today." Granted, I chose a signal more often employed on loading docks than in bedrooms—though if it comes to that—no, the context is all wrong.

By confession's end, I was hurt and angry, as I knew I would be if she insisted on seeing it through. Hurt and angry as I was, I asked if she'd managed to get herself pregnant or just 'Baby Pro' pregnant. Hurt and confused, she called me mean. Just plain angry, I'd told her she could go immolate herself and rise from her own ashes in some junior vice-president for marketing's bed. Just plain hurt, she gathered her things from the bathroom and from the dresser drawer I'd emptied out for her and left.

And now Huang had gone and given me a mirror with the image I'd been trying my damnedest to put out of mind these last two weeks. I couldn't blame him: I hadn't confined my viewing to the reverse side as he instructed. Had the Goddess who made the mirror for me known that I wouldn't follow Huang's instructions? Was such foreknowledge the source of her disillusionment?

I took the mirror from my desk and tried to stare down the skeleton. He didn't blink. What would I do if he beckoned to me as Phoenix-Peggy had? There wasn't much point in wondering. Mr. Bones was nothing if not impassive. Who could guess what he was thinking? And if, by mirror logic, he was thinking what I was thinking, or, by the same mirror logic, he was thinking the reverse of what I was thinking, then, I asked myself, was I staring at my skeletal twin? This seemed no more likely than the possibility that I was looking at some version of myself whenever I saw Phoenix-Peggy's kisser in the other side of the mirror. I spooked myself by wondering how long it would take before I tried to pass Alice-like through the mirror and into the looking-glass equivalent of a Grateful Dead concert attended by Hell's Angels—all death's heads and black leather. I returned the mirror away to my desk drawer.

"Kimono's Japanese." I overheard Judy saying.

"Who made you foreign fashion expert?" Marge from accounts said.

"I'm telling you. It's Chinese wear that jacket."

"And how do you know?"

"I watch the Jackie Chan."

"Go change your filters, Judy."

"Least I know a kimono from a jacket in the Jackie Chan. Hey, Mr. Warner, what's with the little Chinese guy in the silk jacket?"

"You mean Huang? I thought he was Italian."

Marge and Judy in unison: "Italian! Didn't you see how short he was?"

"From where I stood, he looked to be of average height," Dave Warner said.

"Average height!" Marge and Judy again. "For who?"

"What?"

"For Chinese? For Italian? Which?"

"Should we be having this sort of discussion in the workspace?"

"I'm sorry, but that man is tiny!" Judy said.

"She's right, Dave," Marge says, "The man's tiny and that's not going to change whether we say it here in the workspace or downstairs in the garage where you park that abortion on wheels you're so proud of driving."

"Hey!" Dave Warner said.

"If he were a woman, every man in this office would be calling him 'china doll' in no time," Judy said. "You know she's right about that car of yours, Mr. Warner."

Flustered, Dave Warner drew the line: "Ladies, I think we'd better end this conversation before any of us says something that all of us will regret later."

I was at lunch when Phoenix-Peggy left a message on voice-mail. She said she'd been cleaning out her night table drawer and found a souvenir photograph of the two of us taken at the water park the previous summer. She said we looked so happy then and the thought of how happy we'd been made her miss me. She said she was sorry about the night with the junior vice-president for marketing. She said she had forgiven me for the simulated pregnancy crack that had hurt so much because she thought I had said it to belittle her and the company of which she felt so proud to be a part. Then she launched into the Baby Pro sales spiel, sure sign that her boss was monitoring her call.

I should mention that Baby Pro's new product line had been a colossal success with women in love with the idea of being pregnant but who did not want to or could not bring a child into the world. The simulated pregnancy kits came in nine-, eighteen-, and twenty-seven-month versions as well as a trial size that included enough "fertility agent" to carry the curious would-be expectant mother through the first month of morning-sickness-free simulated pregnancy. Top-of-the-line kits came complete with the "Baby's Kickin'" simulator, the "Oops, My Water Broke" simulator, and authentic-looking ultrasound and prenatal testing results.

I had my doubts about Baby Pro and not simply because of its penchant for filling their junior executive corps with malefactors and degenerates. I'd grown suspicious of their entire line as a result after having witnessed Phoenix-Peggy's terrible reaction to a product of theirs then under development. Some month's back, her boss had encouraged some of the younger gals in her office, including Phoenix-Peggy, to take the prototype home with them for the weekend. The women signed a waiver affirming that they hadn't any history of pulmonary trouble or monstrous births.

At the time, I couldn't understand why offering herself up as a guinea pig in exchange for the health risks associated with an experimental product appealed to Phoenix-Peggy and I told her so. As long as we'd been together, she'd never expressed the desire to have a baby or to get pregnant. Hadn't she always insisted that she wanted to focus on her career and that she wanted to wait until we were married before she took the plunge into motherhood? Hadn't she always insisted that she was only twenty-nine, that she still had plenty of fertile years left? She'd nodded assent to both points and said: "I just want to see if this will make my boobs bigger. Baby Pro is thinking about marketing it as a breast enlargement regime also."

She withdrew a small white pouch from a small white box and opened the seal: inside were seven foil packets each bearing the Baby Pro 'Nursin' Mommy' logo and containing two capsules, one red, one blue.

Before I could tell her that I liked her the way she was, she said: "I know, Ken. I know. This is only about me. I'll try it for a week."

"Well, if you know what you're doing…," I couldn't think of a way to end my sentence. She sat down at the dining room table to read the instruction booklet.

After three days, I hadn't noticed any change, though in bed that night Phoenix-Peggy told me that her breasts felt a little tender. I said she should stop taking the capsules and see a doctor. Two nights later, just before I turned off the lamp next to the bed, Phoenix-Peggy pulled up her nightgown and leaned back on her pillow. Baby Pro chemistry hadn't simply augmented her breasts; these looked full to bursting. Her nipples were swollen and her areolas had grown from Nilla wafers into small saucers. Their light pink hue had given way to those darker shades more often observed during the early stages of a black eye. The scent of non-dairy creamer hung about her.

Phoenix-Peggy kept her word. She had signed on to follow the regime for seven days and now the week was out. The following day she came home with a long questionnaire about her experience with Baby Pro's "Nursin' Mommy" kit. She gave the product high ratings as part of a total pregnancy simulation. She seemed less enthusiastic about its prospects as a breast enlargement regime.

So was I. On a new mother, Phoenix-Peggy's new breasts would have been beautiful in a way that only the breasts of a new mother are beautiful. But she wasn't a new mother and her new breasts weren't beautiful in that way. A shudder traveled up and down the length of my spine, shrill herald of some inexpressible loss. Gone was my lover's sense of Phoenix-Peggy's body. When we made love that weekend, I felt as if I were cheating on her with someone else. To the best of my knowledge, Baby Pro's "Nursin' Mommy" Kit is still under development.

Before the seminar, Huang asked me if I'd tried out the mirror. I said I had but did not tell him that I had disobeyed his instructions.

"Very good," he said. "Today and then two more days and Ken the Bear will experience peace for the first time in a long time."

"As long it gets so I can sleep through the night."

"You will sleep through the night, Ken the Bear. And on all succeeding nights you will sleep through the night."

"Sounds great, Huang."

"Let us see who else I can help, Ken the Bear."

Huang moved to the front of the room. From beneath the podium he lifted a large red box with yellow characters and set it down on a table beside a water pitcher and some plastic cups. He raised the lid of the box until it stood straight up and made a vertical plane that would block our view of whatever he lifted out of the box. Huang looked at us the way a magician looks at his audience before he pulls a rabbit from his hat. He reached both hands deep into the box and raised them again until over the top edge of the raised lid there began to appear little moving stars, comets, planets, crescent moons, full moons, a miniature universe of tiny celestial bodies rising as over the horizon. Each little moon, star, planet, and comet crowned a long red strip of see-through plastic. Each springy strip rose from the wide red band that Huang lifted and secured over his dark curls. A little universe danced like a nice field in light wind.

Huang took a small drum from out his briefcase. He chanted as he walked to each corner of the conference room, accompanying himself on the drum. Whenever he reached a corner, he would cease chanting and drumming and stand for several moments in what appeared to be silent meditation. Then the drumming and chanting would start up again as Huang moved on to the next corner. When he completed his circuit of the room, he returned the drum to his briefcase and took out a finger gong which he brushed to alert us that the meeting was about to begin.

"I thank you for coming today. I am Huang. In case you were wondering, it is customary to purify the chamber of illumination through an ancient rite. You will all be good students now I think." Huang laughed hard and the tiny universe over his head shook with approval.

"Corporate, as you know, has sent me to help you implement the changes required by the adoption of the new calendar. Corporate expects everyone to adapt to these changes at a reasonable rate, though resistance is to be expected. Resistance is even useful. The byword at corporate these days is Patience. In the *I Ching*, the characters corresponding to this byword are Compassion Spring." Huang touched the keyboard on his laptop and power-pointed the characters onto the screen behind him. "There is a second byword making the rounds at corporate, one whose characters may be translated as 'After Patience Comes Swift Kick in Ass.'" On the screen: a little man in a suit, bent over, hands on knees, eyes tightly shut, bracing himself against the imminent application of a giant boot to his posterior.

Laughter.

"I now invite questions," Huang said.

"Could you spell out some of the changes you just mentioned?" Juana Durant from creative asked.

"All will be revealed at the proper time."

"What should we do till then?" Vince Carbon from sales asked.

"Breathe deeply. Strive to achieve openness." Huang paused. "Neither of these two activities costs corporate money incidentally."

Laughter.

"Change must be introduced gradually. Each new day will bring change, but not I hope too much. Your managers and I have decided upon a pace that we think will be neither too slow nor too fast."

"How long do we have to get all of this done?" Ellie Wilikers from human resources asked.

"We have until the 22nd of September, the fifteenth day of the eighth lunar month, being the anniversary of the bright goddess's birth. On that evening, we will celebrate the Festival of the Eighth Moon."

"Five and a half weeks doesn't sound like much time to me," Harv Weinstein from graphic design piped in.

"I assure you, it is neither too little nor too much time," Huang said.

Harv Weinstein again: "In that case I would like to make a request."

"I only hope it is within my power to grant."

"Can I try on your hat?"

Bryan Redding from graphic design covered his mouth as if to cough and bellowed "Haaaaarv."

Huang, smiling, spread his arms wide and gestured for Harv to come forward.

Shouts of "You go, Harv."

Steve Wondrus said into the wall phone: "Send up Roger and Cho with camcorders." Then, to the rest of us, "Nobody leave. Nobody move until Roger and Cho get here."

Everyone, including Huang and Harv, remained as they were until Roger and Cho arrived. Roger and Cho set up and gave the sign for action. Huang lifted the dancing headdress and placed it upon Harv's big head. Harv rolled his eyes toward the ceiling as if he could see the stars shimmying above him. Huang let out a great laugh and clapped his hands holding them together for several seconds before spreading his arms wide again and clapping his hands together again.

About half the office's temps entered the room carrying trays of big white cakes shaped like the various phases of the moon. The other half followed with trays of hot tea. All the temps wore dresses of painted silk. They seemed to have no trouble cultivating the slightly arch air mastered long ago by hostesses at your better Chinese restaurants. The moon cakes disappeared quickly. Here and there, the odd red bean or crumb of lotus seed paste adhered to a moist lip. Some employees balked at tea. The temps urged the steaming beverage on them anyway.

Huang nodded at everyone and smiled. He lifted his headdress from Harv's large head and put it on again. As he walked back to his seat, Harv pumped a fist in the air. Everyone laughed and applauded. Huang laughed and applauded. I noticed Huang was wearing red silk slippers trimmed with gold thread.

Back at my cubicle, I had a strong urge to call Phoenix-Peggy. I remembered the mirror and took it from my desk drawer. I followed Huang's exact instructions. Mr. Bones shook his head no.

Huang had been with us less than two weeks when the changes began in earnest. The office was much quieter now. Huang replaced the central cooling units with lead-weight-activated ceiling fans. After a day-long audibility workshop, conversations around the office rarely rose above the level of a stage whisper. Phones in the office no longer bleated as incoming calls were signaled by three chimes whose sequence rendered the concept "Moon" in Chinese musical notation.

The following Monday, Huang presented every employee with a custom pair of slippers—he'd gotten everyone's shoe sizes from human resources—and while the red silk jacket and trousers sported each day by Huang now had not caught on with the men, more and more women in the office were opting for stylish silk and satin dresses. A lunch time fashion-show presented by Ada

Fong of New Moon Fashions was all it had taken. While many of the women had begun to put their hair up with lacquered chopsticks even before Mrs. Chao of Black Jade Studios conducted a makeover seminar, since the session they seemed to be using more face powder. The fragrance of choice around the office was called Jasmine Garden. Many of the women have begun to adopt a small-stepped gait verging on a shuffle. Though they insisted that they were comfortable in their new footwear, I caught Gina Fornato weeping in her cubicle. Still in slippers, she was tugging on what looked like a silk bandage wrapped tightly about her foot.

By midweek, Huang replaced the coffee and soda machines with tea breaks twice at day. Judy grumbled at first about being put in charge of the tea service—it had been easier changing coffee filters a few times a day—but she quieted down after a few words from Huang. Actually, I wondered that there weren't more complaints about the switch to tea. A story told me by Stan Kepling from copywriting went some way toward explaining why. It seems that as soon as Gary Sordquist, another copywriter arrived at the office the other morning with two Starbuck's *muy-grandes,* word came downstairs that the big boss wanted to see him. Gary took a big gulp from one of the containers before setting off upstairs. A little later, Stan's manager called everyone into the conference room and said that Gary was off to corporate to work on a new campaign and that he might be gone for some time.

When the copyrighters returned to their workspace, the Starbuck's has vanished from Gary's desk along with all signs of Gary. When Stan called Gary at home that evening, Gary's wife answered sounding frightened and upset. She managed get out that Gary couldn't come to the phone before breathing in sharply the way people do after they've been crying a lot. Stan tried calling Gary several more times without success.

The other day, I went down to the fifth floor to see if Don in coding wanted to join me for a quick one after work. He hadn't replied to my emails, but Don was a busy guy. Though I'd visited him hundreds of times before, I was lost even before I stepped off the elevator. Nothing looked familiar except the large □ painted on the facing wall. Don and a dozen other programmers wrote code in a big windowless room crammed with PCs. To keep the hardware from overheating, Don and his mates kept their workspace several degrees cooler than any other room in our building. You knew you were getting close when a draught of cold air slapped you like the blast from an ice-cream truck freezer as you passed the adjoining hallway. But no arctic chill was forthcoming and after a fruitless search, I started trying every door. I opened the last door of the third hallway upon a hundred men in silk jackets and silk trousers and deep concentration. Each scribe sat at a knee-high table with his legs folded beneath him. Each scribe brandished a fine-pointed brush. The room was silent but for the sound of brushstrokes on rice paper and a small fountain whose pool was fringed with delicate bamboo.

No one looked up from their writing. No one said anything. Not even a dismissive "May I help you?" The scribes continued to apply their brushstrokes as if I weren't there. "Anyone seen Don?" I asked. Nothing. "Don?" I repeated. I left the chamber of echoes and climbed the steps back to my own floor in silence.

At the end of the second week, Huang announced that corporate wanted to reward all of us for our hard work. For two hours every afternoon until the lunar festival, we would be free to devote ourselves to supervised contemplation and spiritual exercises. At great expense, corporate had flown in Huang's own teacher to instruct us. Out of regard for our tight schedule, Master Lin had even agreed to conduct a four-hour introductory class that afternoon. Huang failed to mention that Master Lin's burly assistants carried staves of hardest oak which they would not scruple to apply to the back or legs of any employee who tried to mask his or her disobedience with mental distraction and physical fatigue. When some of the older and out-of-shape began to protest, Huang called class with more than an hour left in the session. He apologized and said he would personally explain to Master Lin's assistants how things worked in corporate America. He begged us not to blame Master Lin for his overzealous disciples.

Huang did not attend class the next day. His word with the Master's assistants might have done some good. While the beatings commenced almost at once, they didn't last as long. On the other hand, their brief duration did nothing to mitigate their brutality. Another week and the number of participants had dwindled to less than half our original complement. Assistants disappeared as Master Lin grew more pleased with the progress of the remaining students. He rarely called us dogs anymore. We learned not to inquire after those who had stopped showing up. One of the last to have his named scratched off the class roster showed up late one night at St. Bodo's hospital with brain injuries. The doctors watched him slip into a coma and he was now in the care of a head trauma nurse whose wife's cousin worked at branch.

I was still reaping the benefits of Huang's mirror cure. Mr. Bones was still glaring at me whenever I looked his way. Each time I peeked into the other side of the mirror, the image of Phoenix-Peggy appeared to grow fainter like the fading likeness of Dorothy's Auntie Em in witch-green Margaret Hamilton's crystal ball. Of course, Auntie Em had been calling Dorothy's name and holding her hand to her chest out of worry, fear, and heartache. Phoenix-Peggy stared out at me looking, well… I could see through her. I broke down and called her at work.

Her voice-mail chirped that Phoenix-Peggy was away from her desk, but I got hold of Amy Knoblach who worked in the same department. Amy said that Phoenix-

Peggy had been resting at her mothers since undergoing a grueling series of medical tests earlier this week. She said I could reach her there and that a call from me might do Phoenix-Peggy good. She said Phoenix-Peggy had been meaning to call me, but that she had felt too ravaged to pick up a phone. "I'll let her tell you the rest herself," Amy said.

Phoenix-Peggy's voice sounded weak when she answered the phone but she insisted that we talk. She'd felt terribly ill for weeks but had tried to wait it out. Only when her breasts hardened and her nipples cracked did she grow scared enough to seek medical attention. The first doctor had been cruel and joked that Phoenix-Peggy should not plan on dancing topless soon. She'd wept in his office and on the drive home and now she was beginning to weep again. The doctor had scored a direct hit on the lightly-ballasted vessel of her self-esteem, one buoyed by her sense of herself as a free spirit, and sent it shattered and whirling to the bottom. Uncovered, her breasts had stood for the healthy abandon and guiltless sexuality that she had always tried to carry off without—or so I had thought—much success.

To be fair—and I wanted to be fair and even generous to her at this moment for all the moments when I'd been neither fair nor generous to her, for all the moments when I'd been as callous and unkind as her doctor—she'd succeeded far more often than I would have admitted. I wanted to tell her how she'd well shed carried it off and how I might have been able to tell her so back when we were still together had I been less churlish and selfish and stupid. I told her how sorry I was.

She said that the doctors still weren't sure but they thought that the prototype Baby Pro 'Nursin' Mommy Kit' had triggered an allergic reaction. She said that the cortisone injections hadn't done any good but at least the doctors had put her on pain-killers so that she'd been able to sleep. Back at work, I peeked into the wrong side of the mirror again. Phoenix-Peggy's translucent flesh was the color of ash. Her eyes emitted only palest light.

Midway through his tenure at branch, Huang gathered everyone into the large conference room. His manner was grave. "I have sad news for everyone. One of your colleagues has seen fit to act against the good of the whole." The doors opened and an accountant named Gig Mallard stumbled into the room as if pushed from behind by one of Master Lin's assistants. He kneeled before us. Master Lin's assistant fell in behind him, loomed over him. Gig Mallard spoke: "I hereby confess to stealing from petty cash." A sharp blow to the back of his head staggered him. "From the common stock, I mean. I have made restitution and I now ask your forgiveness."

Huang added coldly: "The criminal understands that your forgiveness will not save him from punishment. He repents his crime and craves your forgiveness."

"You said all I had to do was confess, pay back the cash, and ask their forgiveness," Gig Millard said.

"No. I said that in return for your willingness to comply with these measures, you would receive swift punishment." On Huang's signal, Gig Mallard was escorted from the conference room by Master Lin's disciple with the help of Doug Watkins from community outreach. We heard no more about Gig's fate until the following week when his widow arrived at human resources to discuss his life insurance policy and his pension plan.

Her mother called to tell me that the seizures had stopped but that Peggy had been transferred from St. Bodo's to Glade Manor, a nursing home reserved for the destitute. Citing unauthorized private use of an experimental product, Baby Pro had refused to pay for Peggy's care and treatment. At first, Mrs. Schnitzler had made up the shortfall out of her own pocket. But private hospital costs being what they were, she was running out of money fast. A hospital administrator arranged for her to place Peggy under Glade Manor's care at the public's expense, Residual toxins in her system had left Peggy confused and weak. Some days she couldn't remember what had happened to her. I asked Mrs. Schnitzler if she thought Peggy would like a visit from me. She said she would ask her. She said I shouldn't expect anything, that this Peggy was very changed from the Peggy I'd known. In lieu of goodbye, Mrs. Schnitzler said how proud Peggy had always been of her figure.

I pocketed the mirror and set off for Huang's temporary offices on the ninth floor. If the mirror had somehow contributed to Phoenix-Peggy's condition, if the damage might be reversed, I had a right to know. I made my way past the flower-covered gate and down the narrow hallway with a marble screen at its halfway point. From carved beams that ran the length of the passage's ceiling hung cages of finches, thrushes, wrens, and other songbirds. On the other side of the screen, I saw a large court hemmed in by painted columns. An old man wrapped in black silk admitted me through a hidden door and I followed him onto a terrace. Huang was studying a large astronomical chart that traced the moon's orbit. Beside him stood an ancient-looking astronomer calculating lunar trajectories with an abacus. When he saw me he nodded and sent the astronomer away: "I can see, Ken the Bear, that your soul has been restored to the path to health."

"I wanted to ask to you about that. I've been looking in the reverse side of the mirror like you told me to—though sometimes I looked into the other side too."

Huang shook his head as if pretending to scold me then smiled. "Of course what you have done will not always yield the most desired result, Ken the Bear, but you feel better nevertheless."

"I do, but—"

"—but you are concerned about one whose image appears in the wrong side of the mirror and you think the mirror is somehow responsible for her decline. I ask you, Ken the Bear: was she concerned about you when she turned unfaithful?"

"You know about that?"

"Was she concerned about you when she invited another man into her bed?"

"Is she going to die?"

"It is not for me to say. The mirror's power is strong, Ken the Bear, but if she dies it will not be the fault of the mirror. I am sorry. I may concern myself only with the health of friends and of those who depend on me."

"If you could see how much she has suffered…"

"I am sorry. I can do nothing for her."

"At least take your mirror back."

"I cannot take back what was never mine. I cannot take from you what is yours."

"I don't want her to die."

"It is not up to you."

"Who is it up to then?"

"It is not for me to say. I am sorry, Ken the Bear but it is now time for you to go."

With the lunar celebrations less than a week away, Huang made a big announcement. New offices awaited us across town and buses waiting downstairs would take us to them. We would occupy the top floor of the seventy-three storey Lunar Arts Tower complete with the newly finished Moon Terrace. A glass skylight in place of most of the ceiling would provide us with an unobstructed view of the night sky.

Huang followed the big announcement with others less winning. Traditional dress would now be mandatory for all employees. We would receive a supply of good brushes and ink. The use of PCs, pens and pencils would henceforth be prohibited. We would be expected to attend a seminar entitled Ancient Chinese Calligraphy for Dummies in the great conference hall. On Sunday evening, new hours of operation would take effect. Work would begin at 9PM and end at 5AM. All changes were to be considered permanent until further notice.

Mrs. Schnitzler called to say that if I meant to visit Peggy I should probably get to Glade Manor sooner than later. She said she was praying for a miracle.

"Think she'll recognize me?"

"Hard to say, Kenny. Hard to say if you'll recognize her. She's so changed."

The mirror had gone missing. I looked for it under a pile of memos marked "urgent" and checked the desk drawer again to no avail. Co-workers had begun rehearsing the lunar incantations in small groups. I ducked into the elevator and caught the 2:10 bus to Glade Manor only to learn that Peggy had been sent back to St. Bodo's for an emergency tracheotomy. I was back at my desk within the hour. An inter-office envelope was waiting for me. The box for the sender had been left blank. I didn't bother to check for a note. I retrieved the mirror and locked it away in my desk.

At lunch the next day, Josh Dembowski from compliance told me about a pair of binoculars that belonged to Huang. Transmitted into each lens was a different live image. In the right lens, the viewer saw the most distant object in the universe, a dying star in the galaxy called X2HΨB as revealed by the most powerful telescope in the world. In the left lens, the viewer saw the universe's smallest object—nobody could say what it was for sure—revealed by the most powerful electron microscope in the world. It seems that one of the flower maidens tried the binoculars when Huang stepped out. When she tried to return them to his desk, she missed the desk by a mile. Huang came back to find the binoculars on the floor but undamaged.

The flower maiden seemed to be rehearsing a bizarre new dance in which her feet despaired of ever finding the floor again. Huang ordered her out of the office, but her steps were so tentative that she still hadn't reached the door half an hour later. Huang's special binoculars caused her to lose all sense of distance: she could no longer tell how close or far she was from anyone or anything else.

I've tried to stop looking into the mirror, afraid of what I might see. The other night, I dreamt that I'd purposely dropped it off a bridge only to find it back on my desk the following morning. I've thought of losing it on the bus that takes me to and from Phoenix-Peggy's nursing home, but I'm convinced that it will find its way back. I simply have to stop looking into it ever again. Red banners welcoming the Eighth Moon have now appeared throughout the office and on the Moon Terrace.

Preparations for tomorrow's lunar festival were nearly complete by the time I showed up for work tonight. I'd arrived half an hour late and received a typically severe warning from one of Master Lin's assistants: a deafening box on the ears. It would have done no good to tell him that I'd been late because I'd been visiting Phoenix-Peggy. Her mother had been right to wonder if I would recognize her. Victim of terrible change she was unresponsive and seemed beyond help. I thought to take her hand, but her hand had frozen into a claw. I thought to tell her that I'd forgiven her, that I still loved her. I thought to ask for her forgiveness, for her love. It was no use: something told me that I was to blame for all her suffering. I left her bedside and headed back to the office.

Huang assembled everyone for the last time two hours before the Festival of the Eighth Moon was scheduled to commence. He told us how proud corporate was of us. He told us to give ourselves a round of applause and our applause soon turned into the sort of rhythmic clapping you'd expect to hear at the Beijing Opera. Huang began to run through some last minute details. I'd stopped listening by then.

Earlier, I'd followed my own worst advice and gazed into the reverse side of the mirror for what was to be the last time. The skeleton was gone. With something like last hope, I flipped the mirror over to search the glass for Phoenix's image. Phoenix was gone too. The mirror had told me everything I needed to know, but I caught the next bus back Glade Manor anyway. I got there just in time to watch a nurse strip the bedding from Phoenix-Peggy's mattress to get it ready for the next terminal case.

I'm not sure why I bothered going back to the office that night. I must have figured that since Phoenix had been sacrificed, I might as well get a good look at the Goddess for whom she'd died.

Out on the Moon Terrace, strange music played. From a rampart, I gazed down at the mobbed streets below. Even from this height I could make out dancers steering a great yellow dragon with poles to mimic the river spirit's sinuous windings. Then came a procession of eunuchs hoisting banners with gold and silver fish, twirling parasols adorned with painted butterflies and blossoms, and waving great fans of peacock and pheasant plumes. The eunuchs had accompanied the Presidential Concubine on the long journey from the Capital. The great personage herself came into view borne aloft in a gold sedan chair by eight massive bearers who maintained a dignified pace all the way to the entrance of the Lunar Arts Building. A less stately approach was out of the question since well-wishers carrying flowers and gifts insisted on running into the path of that amply-cushioned carriage and right up to the traveling chair itself.

In the Courtesan-in-Chief's wake, pallid color-guardsmen shouldered furled ensigns and pressed dully on against night's advance. With each stride they covered less ground and in no time their once quick steps had slowed to a funeral march. Behind them, a dozen robed men, moved forward in loose array, waving pennants emblazoned with the likeness of a phoenix encircled in a wreath of flames. They sang words from an old poem set to older music:

The Phoenix play on their terrace.
The Phoenix are gone.
On and alone the river flows.
The Moon haunts their terrace.
The Phoenix are gone.

The appearance of the imaged flock was no less ghastly for my having blamed it on ghastly coincidence. In my bewilderment I leapt at the first available means of writing off so unequivocal a sign. Afterwards, I was only dimly aware of the painted phoenixes winging their way toward me through hoops of fire.

Mental shock waves abridged the contents of my mind even as they readjusted its default focus settings to high blur. I'd stumbled upon conclusive evidence for the mind's unlimited capacity for fucking with itself and arrived at this horrible understanding: even in its most vacant and muddled state, my mind remained the mightiest of receivers and the subtlest of tuners for picking up those lowest of the low-end frequencies assigned to grief.

That's right, cichos and chichas. You're tuned to W-O-E. We're talking way past rock bottom on your brain-radio dial. [Sound effect: Someone saying "OOOPS!" followed by the sound of a cherished and irreplaceable article being dropped into the abyss followed by the sound of said article falling endlessly through empty space.] This just in. Memo to Ken the Bear from the Goddess of Disillusion and Mr. Bones. Re: Phoenix Update. Dear Ken, Phoenix is still dead. All reports of her resurrection are greatly exaggerated. [Sound effect: sound of foghorn sounding like the deep cry of a great lonesome beast, more lament than call, followed by the sound of an empty sea where no ships come.] Ouch! That's gotta hurt. Still, everyone loves the

Goddess. And, oh, that Mr. Bones. We all know how he gets sometimes. Hey, Ken the Bear. Bet you didn't remember the phrase that pays. Now, listen up cuz I'll only gonna say it once. W-O-E is me! Hope you got it that time, Ken the Bear. [Sound effect: sound of an irate Grizzly bellowing hot in pursuit of prey followed by sound of an old lady, fleeing, out of breath, saying "Oh my!" followed by sound of man saying "You kids seen Grandma?"] OK, but this is absolutely the last time: W-O-E is me! It's the praise that sways. The gaze that preys. And speaking of the phase that flays, why don't we go to Huang over at the Moon Terrace for tonight's lunar report. Come in, Huang. Ground Control to Major Huang. What's that? No, Miss Helen Pomeroy of the Woonsocket Board of Health, I certainly did not say that. You've got to lay off those Lifetime Movies for Women. Huang? Huang, are you there? Houston, we have an issue: Major Huang appears to have left the capsule. And he's floating in a most peculiar way...

"The stars look very different today," Huang said. "Ken the Bear, I am so happy to see that you are joining us on the Moon Terrace."

"I'm not staying." Huang searched my eyes for a clue in the ruby light that drifted down to us from a sea surface of paper lanterns hanging overhead. I stayed focused, determined not to give anything away. I'd guessed he'd be too proud or too fearful to ask straight out and I was right. He drew his lips together into a faint smile, lowering and lifting his chin in a way that fell short of a nod. After long silence, Huang rejoined the dignitaries on the viewing stand.

The last verses of the lunar incantations were capped off with a fireworks display. By the time the smoke cleared, the bright goddess had begun her progress across the sky.

From the streets below rose the chorus of the Hymn to the Eighth Moon. The voices of everyone around me on the rooftop joined the voices from below. All over the city, bells rang and sirens wailed. The Eighth Moon was shining her mythic light upon all her children above and upon all her children below.

I couldn't be party to all that lunar joy any longer. I made my way downstairs to the great window at the far side of the office for one more look at the churning streets below. The silence of the throng rose even to this height. The sky brightened immeasurably and against my brow I felt a strange pressure, the hand of an evangelist dripping with grace like clover honey. I turned my back to the glass in time to watch the far wall drenched in blinding light. When my sight returned, I saw my own shadow, sole prisoner in all that radiance, frozen in arctic whiteness. To spring him I only had to walk across the office to where the Moon could not invoke her ancestral right to gaze upon whomever or whatever she pleased.

I met the lunar incarcerate at the edge of dark and light, gave him his liberty, and crossed the border. I waited a moment to see if the moon would her press ancient prerogative. But except for the glow that filled the entire office on the other side of the line—a warning no doubt— the moon offered no further shows of force. I recalled the custom of freeing one prisoner on royal anniversaries.

Once more, I made my way to my desk. I unlocked its drawer and pulled it open. The mirror had vanished as I had expected it would.

I was waiting at reception for the ink on my resignation to dry when a fax from corporate arrived: a consultant would shortly arrive to help branch implement the new health plan. I heard the hum of an ascending elevator car and the chime signaling that it had reached our floor. The doors slid open and the new consultant stepped out. He was wearing a grotesquely carved ebony mask. In his right hand, he held the bloody carcass of a rooster; in his left hand, a sack of vipers.

RIVER BLINDNESS

(Poems)

"WHAT'S THE FREQUENCY, KENNETH?"

After many months, the cameramen grew
indifferent and began filming anything
that resembled action. Each episode ran

a week or more, revealing a few minutes
of the hero's life, so most of our time
was spent in keeping objects at rest,

in observing the guidelines for change.
Sometimes we failed, and, in an otherwise
happy scene, a flourishing african

violet might wither inexplicably,
or the brightly colored wallpaper might
fade without warning. Moments like these

always disquieted us like the muted
conversations heard through hotel walls,
or carried into our rooms by the obscure

waves of a distant radio. "So you found him
this time but maybe you won't be so lucky
the next. After all this haystack isn't

getting any smaller. And what makes you so
sure you got the right guy anyway, genius?"
Was what they desired something they

desired for itself, or was it only part
of some larger scheme, only hinted at
in the dimmest signals, and dark to most

of us, a secret as deep as the silence
left by the flight of cranes. There's not
much we can know actually. Even so, we

always seem to find ourselves turning over
stones in other people's gardens, or peering
into strange archways. We really shouldn't

trouble ourselves. The man in the raincoat isn't
talking yet. And were he, would we be ready
for the knowledge he had to impart?

Perhaps it's better we don't answer the phone
every time it rings, better we leave a few
letters unopened-half-measures but sincere,

part of an effort to keep things close,
to let some things pass quietly through
the ravening net of inquiry.

To live without all these questions,
that would be repose-and yet not quite,
since there would always be those thoughts

surfacing like the fossil remains of some
delicate creature, dislodging themselves
from the sheer rock face of the past

after a thousand centuries of rough weather.
Of course, we'd have to get beyond this
if things were ever going to return

to normal, if we were ever going to be
able to trace our own shallow footprints
back to the shore where each evening

we'd wait for the music from the lake
pavilions to find us happy and at rest
in the tall grasses, even as another

music, more ancient, unheard, drifted far
above us, and beguiled the astronomers,
and set the ritual stones to song.

DREAM FOX

Not the five tiny black birds that new
out from behind the mirror
over the washstand,
nor the raccoon that crept
out of the hamper,
nor even the opossum that hung
from the ceiling fan
troubled me half so much as
the fox in the bathtub.

There's a wildness in our lives.
We need not look for it.
That's wrong too.
It finds us.

It finds us,
naked and alone,
in unfamiliar bathrooms,
wiping the grit from our eyes,
waiting for the first signs
that we're back among the living.

I catch him beneath his forelegs and lift.
"Don't bite me," I say. Says he, "I'll bite you."

MALVINAS ECLOGUE, 1995

Corin: A Young Shepherd. Lassie: His Dog.

Lassie: I'll not be going to that field again.
Three more of Willie's flock and two of Thom's
exploded yesterday—a wooly blast.
I almost lost a paw myself last week.

Corin: I shouldn't ask you. No, my dear? I'd not
have you stain your coat of fawn crawling
through barbed wire nor lose you to a landmine
buried years ago by some savage Brit or Argentine.

Lassie: Happy the man and dog, whose wish and care
a few untroubled, sheep-shorn acres bound,
whose peaceful fires blaze and warm the night.
Nights, I lie awake and think about the past.

SMOKE SIGNALS

The treaty paddled
far up the Missouri
until it reached
the long-distance tribes.

Lately they'd begun
to screen their calls.
Maybe they'd pick up
but wouldn't speak.

Maybe we'd hear them
whisper a little
to one another
as the line went dead.

Many moons later,
after we Wiled-Out®
their creepy names
in our black books,

the strangest blue wisps
appeared above the mesa.
Had they whipped up some
new kind of weather?

We pieced together
a dusky message:
Happy-here-at-last-
alone-with-buffalo.

An invite. What we'd
waited for. Was there
another way to take
so cloudy a sign?

MY MEMORY OF HAVING STARRED

Last night I dreamt I was the Supremes.
I was beautiful in my white sequined gowns.

WHAT I LIVE BY

Some jerk once asked me what motto I lived by.
I hate mottoes but mine's "Bad news travels fast."

THEY DRIVE BY NIGHT

In the desert, luminous diners
bloom like neon cactus flowers.

In this radiance,
the counterman
awaits your order.

So you tell him the armadillo chili
with a side of Jerusalem artichokes,

Just as you dig in,
a wrecker appears
in the parking lot.

It's trailing some late-model remains:
fatal accordion stuck on a silent chord.

WHEN THE MOON COMES OUT

When the moon comes out
the chimes cease to sound.
The easiest ways appear
impossible to wend.

When the moon comes out
the seas slip over the globe.
The heart as an isle appears,
her shores by infinity washed.

Oranges none may taste
while the full moon lasts.
Undesired, just within reach,
cold, still green fruit hangs.

When the moon comes out
with her same hundred faces,
pocketfuls of silver,
newly minted, whimper.

MANDELSTAM

The pinewoods burn at night,
burn in the eyes of toy wolves
hidden away in the bushes.

O what sadness sight brings,
O what hidden range —
the frozen arc of heaven,
its endless laughter.

EVGENY ONEGIN 1.31

O, how and to what wilderness exiled,
fool, could you forget their soft approach?
Tiny feet, what wildflowers yield before you,
what tender leaves admit your shy advance?
Orient's child, bred of warmth and mildness,
in stilled fields plastered smooth with snow,
you left no impression, nothing to impress;
but adored the way each silent footfall met
a carpet's coy resistance, a rug's rich embrace.
Is it because of you that I stand here a stone
when in confinement I hear news from home?
No thoughts of fame or leisure stir me now.
My youth is gone, and my joys disappear
as grassy footprints in the gentlest breeze.

SIN-CALF

Far from the sacred precincts, the outcast
lies awake, fears the jackal and the kite.
She tries to remember her lover's face.
Yet even now, a great shadow is sweeping
toward her over the tents and that delicate
mouth which once drew forth another's breath
must yield once more. Only law endures.

ONE FORM HER DOUBT TAKES

She woke to rain falling without pattern.
To hear upon waking was to hear a first time
not the dull incessant rain, not the rain
beating down, bending the new grass,
but the rain stealing, giving nothing.
Her room grew large, became the night,
black-beaded, scented with the reddest blooms
unfolding at midnight in garden darkness.
She felt its soft embrace what she wanted,
merely to be held and not belong. And thought
how something might be saved, a ripeness
beyond summer, red fading only to red,
unperceived at night, rain falling into sleep.

"YOUR HEART WOULD HAVE RESPONDED"

All other ghosts tremble and dissolve
when after longer absence you appear
pacing jagged ridgelines wrapped in mist,
waving from the lake depths ragged in weeds.
Your visits leave me silently unsure
strangely fearful of that greener world
where once or twice I wandered in the light
that falls before the shadows sweep the land.
I found you in a corner of the wood
and though you could not tell me where you'd been,
it seemed you must have come from far away,
glad, once here, to curl up in the leaves,
and certain of discovery, for a time
to close your eyes and wait for my return.

"DAMIEN HIRST'S 'ISOLATED ELEMENTS SWIMMING IN THE SAME DIRECTION FOR PURPOSES OF UNDERSTANDING'"

I only heard about your long shelves full
of small vitrines—so many tideless worlds.
In each a brilliant fish—fin and gill
fixed within an impalpable current—
shines ghostlike in its dank enclosure,
incorruptible in its private sea
of five-percent formaldehyde solution.
These luminous creatures purpose more
than homely understanding. They draw us
deep into a world where no lips press,
no laughter peals, no talk of love disturbs,
where the only sound's a tuneless humming,
and, there, a cold that stops the heart,
and tiny lights that pierce the rippled tide.

"I AM FROM THERE"

How these words curled round, brought me home
when they were only meant to place you there
when from there I would take you as in doubt.

I heard you then as one I loved but did not know,
as one whose love no winter lake could muffle
ashore in shore pine or low cloud or fastness,

With these you took me home as if from home
and set me down by you as by the quietest fire
that embered in the flush of your indignation.

RIVER BLINDNESS

We slept late that spring, backs to the dawn,
but heard the tree frogs singing in their cages,
and the cries of the waterfowl on the river,
waking only to discover the night clouds
already headed for the northern peaks
to linger there unsure of their own portents.
If the weather would not counsel us, then what
would commend our future, what happen then
to the homemade signs long grown familiar,
to the tell-tale symptoms we'd counted on
for warmth even as they dwindled, certain,
as we were, they'd come back to us someday
like those tiny alpine blooms that one or twice
an age peek out at us from under their glacier.

O, we'd already begun
to miss the brighter days with their festivals,
their bannered vessels full of fresh stores
arriving as they always did at twilight,
coming into view just as the first fires
of the evening appeared beside the waters,
signal to our merchants that they were home
and would soon find rest in their own beds
undisturbed by tempests or strange tongues.
Just last week, we returned from the provinces
disappointed that our favorite vistas
had lost their charm. At first, we blamed it
on the light, but knew that something else
had come between us and the old terrain,
and separated us from the sorts of places
whose names are forgotten before their
hold on us begins to wane, though even then
the local mood may survive, challenging us

to stay firm in our choices.

Once in a northern country, I held your hand,
clutched it warm inside my coat pocket.
Snow was falling. And I thought there might be
some way to protect and save the season
from the greener months that lay ahead
and promised something new but uninvited.

I'm tired of loss, tired of the way it
turns us back upon ourselves, ourselves,
like a recording of a scratched record playing.

Tonight, wild moonlight haunts
the courtyard and a low wind carries
the scent of fern through an open window.
Our scribes work late into the evening,
and there's comfort in knowing that the lives
preserved in their characters belong to us.

So what if the news from the frontier grows
more dismal each time a shabby messenger
appears at our gate.

Things could be worse.
At least we're not alone, at least we're all
moving toward the same always distant always
near catastrophe, at least there's no one
who'll accept our apologies for the way
things turned out without smiling, without
giving themselves away, without giving us
something of value in return, shining there
in the current, meant only for our eyes.

THE WORST KIND OF TRAFFIC

The road to the airport is filled
with the worst kind of traffic.
We ignore more garish warnings,
but somehow I can't stop thinking
about that dinner at Rudolpho's,
about the waiter with the bad cough,
about the woman who spilled her drink
and laughed about it for the rest of the evening.

OUT OF KILTER

Please. Drive them off with sticks if you must.
Just make them go away. Too many bad draughts
drawn against accounts long expired, our balances
run to zero eons ago.

The first stars appear
seeking instant rapprochement with the last deciders
now winding up their managerial progress down
from the top floors to just below street level,
everyone else in a rush to be there on time
to greet them, here beneath the elevated. Candy,
loose change, evening papers: all lost in the weeds
that clog our way over barely surmountable hills.

For old times sake, just go ahead and loft one high,
high over towers where long girls twist their tresses
like spun cable in the dazzled noon, while far below
a thousand dark-visored, high-booted riders—hoof
beats muffled in sand—course the scorching river bed
past the forsaken estates. And long past, the endless fêtes,
the once interminable galas, ended, all of them, to sounds
of broken glass falling. Even the bejeweled accordions
have stopped their incessant wheezing.

Balance? Love?
What of these? Without a single voice to carry them off
like tin twin trophies at amateur hour, why you'd think—
don't you laugh. I fain would know—don't laugh I said—
what thoughts has she what pass these days for grace,
what thoughts has she of what passes now from grace?

FLIGHT TO SANTIAGO

Evening comes on, a little drunk perhaps;
he's hauling beside him an outsize valise
covered with stars. An overnight bag's draped
over his shoulder. The flight's delayed again.
He's patient though. He knows that day is losing
her grip. She's already left the parks
and the wider avenues. And now she clings
only to the tops of the tallest buildings.
The slightest breeze will send her packing.
He settles in beside you, removes his hat,
and smiles benignly *buenas noches*.
You smile back and say his name *evening*.

Aloft, he takes out of his large wallet
a thousand million wallet-size photographs
of his favorite children, all brilliant:
Andromeda at five teasing Canis Minor,
Ophiuchus bearing his first serpent,
shy Virgo and her date at the junior prom.
My children's eyes shine like the stars he says
forgetting that his children are the stars,
not marking that the eyes of another seated
beside him shine as brightly, not knowing
how those eyes, your eyes, like lodestars, lead me
always home, how that light, your light guides me
always back to you, back to the deep shade
of the night trees where you wait for me
and wait to take your place as a daughter
of the evening among the other stars.
How I long to lose myself once again
in the radiant empires of your night.

JACK ROBERTS

OVER TEMUCO

Over Temuco the night air trembles
with the ghostly trilling of ancient pipes,
with the insipid whining of a bi-plane
headed for the frontier and trouble.

Over Temuco my dream of you hovers,
distressed at the thought of missing you.
In old cantinas with their green awnings,
in the less reputable cafes that line
the Boulevard de las Americas,
in dance halls pulsing with tangos,
my dream of you listens impatiently
for any news of you. And none arrives.

And so for days it follows riverbeds
high into the foothills of the Andes.

It comes to you as wind in the tall grass.
It comes to you as wind across the lake.
It comes to you as wind against the cliffs.
It comes to you as wind through the forest
It comes to you bearing the scent of fern,
of fragrant earth, of vines that bloom at night.

And when at dusk it finds you by a fire,
your face and eyes aglow with firelight,
finds you laughing that easy laugh
that draws all things adoringly to you,
my dream now as a breeze runs its fingers
through the warm dust, stretches out
in the warm dust at your feet, and, as one
who after long thirst deeply drinks, sighs.

THE NEW REFORMS

Those were fluid days. And the wind that met us
as we turned into the street which traced
the line of conquest sang of pleasant rains.

On the steps of the public library,
vendors talked only of the lost caravan.
Then, we thought of you almost constantly.

If there had been an opening, a rent
in the arras, there was no way of knowing.
That night, the martins grew silent in their nests.

In the square the lines began to soften.
and all around us space became something
no longer to be feared. We could see

everything. That was not the problem.
The difficulty lay in seeing further,
beyond what we always saw: the showgirls,

the luncheonettes, the tiny pools themselves
which had never failed until now to waken
all sorts of feelings. These pass from our minds

as one passes from the lobby unobserved
and having found some quieter spot, looks once
around and lights a cigarette. The builders

grow old and move away, leaving no plans
for those who remain; far too damaged
to repair, these walls admit a stranger light,

Our newest maps reflect the coastal changes.

Beneath the shore estates, the rock shifts
another inch; a great cornice falls away.

I follow highways north along the sea,
through mossy headlands verging on the sea.
I am lost and will not know my place again,

carried along by some other power
toward regions of ice; behind me only love
stretched tight as deerskin across continents

And though I could blame the cartographers,
was it their fault they had hoped to create
a landscape untouched by the old failures

that touch us even as we fail so that
it all had the sense of a Hollywood ending.
You know the one I'm thinking of.

It's where the Creature, alone as before,
the blonde girl having been taken from him,
moves off toward the tar pits. He knows even then

he won't be coming back. Slowly submerging,
he takes one last look back—there may be
peace—at the lovely world he is losing.

SIX YEARS ON

The Creature had left
not lost the world.
And the blonde girl
hadn't been taken from him.
He'd driven her off
with too lavish praise,
with a creature-fear
of being seen.

She never even saw him.
Whether in moonlight,
in carnival-light,
in cave-darkness,
he'd hid under words,
angular and massy
like the leather plates
of a tortoise shell.

He's falling now,
fathom after fathom,
down deep into pitch.
The shell cracks.
Then silence. Is this
the desired peace?

He longs for the world again.
He longs for her.

She's sitting
at the edge
of the tar pit.
She's humming
a song to herself.

She's spinning
a rope of dried grass.

INADEQUACY

The word would ring and I interrupted
answer and though unready receive her
but willing (or I thought) that she enter
anyway and stay before not staying.
Always she stood between me and that she
who in fairness she if fair would advance
were love to the one loved adequate
so to that she I might incline and love.
Whether slipped by her on opening or what
now you stand to me now have placed me so
so now her back is turned as I face you
and see you make it so she cannot fail you
should she since I before you only stand
now there where to you alone I adhere.

MARGITSZIGETEN...

The stones of the mined monastery
tremble with a childishly insipid
and, no doubt, immensely popular
television theme launched heavenwards
from a psychedelic mobile phone
whose besotted owner croons his love
to his third last love this week.

Some might call
this profanation, but what's profane
about love and faith. If not his faith,
why not then that of the duskrunners
steps away on the island-ringing path.
Quiet as monks, surely as austere,
these too would home before dark.

Here, on this island, in this double city,
in this behorded, kinged, and sainted country,
all is reconciled. And I am reconciled.

Forty years it's taken me to learn what I need
what another knew in youth and youthful death.
Sándor, your language defies me, denies my own.
And so with you I say: Szabadság, szerelem!
E kettő kell nekem. And love's still love
And freedom just another name for faith.

FOR IMRE NAGY

Unremarkable, like all the others, drab-jacketed,
squinting at us from behind spotless lenses,
your voice wanted resonance, because, put on the spot,
in the urgency to say something, you couldn't think
of what to say to the thousands gathered below,
the sudden need for words, its unexpectedness,
principally, what you accounted strange.
I listened to you, old fellow with pince-nez,
let down, not yet was I to know

about the concrete yard where—it's a good guess—
the state prosecutor spat out the sentence,
about the rope's uncouth grazing, the last disgrace.

Who can say what might have been said
from that balcony? Machine-gunned chances
don't come again. Prison, death: these cannot
whet the moment's blade once the edge
is off. Even so, we're free to remember
the reluctant, wounded, tentative man
up into whom, for all that, was poured
rage, delusion, a nation's blind hopes

when the city woke to shooting
that blew it all apart.

AMERICAN SESTINA: FOURTH OF JULY

Since nobody else will, I'll say it: You really couldn't
have asked for nicer weather.
There. It's said. And it's good to know we can say
things like this without turning
our backs on the quotation-mark-less way to say
things like this when endless series
of mawkish have-a-nice-days, hawkish sing-the-
Lord's-praises quell all felt comment.
It's only fair that we who say: "there but for the gag-
reflex go I" should come at last
to wonder if it weren't high time we all just started
being not being serious enough.

Aren't the mind-numbing numb-minded mal mots of
some presidents serious enough
for all of you? Take a certain zombie governor of a
brother: Said Jebu of the weather
forecasters' ill success as hurricanes shredded Florida
homes like paper summer last:
Presume not the ways of the Lord to know, for
behold! when Jesus feels like turning
a thousand trailer parks into sand and splinters and
strips of tin, that's no comment
on His love but on our sins. Jebu reads to Wubs from
that creepy Left Behind series.

In 1969, a Tulsa lad reacted badly—nausea, chills—to
a pre-camp vaccination series.
Good thing Dad knew his emetics. Plying his darkest
Okie arts, he'd soon enough
concocted Tang, breakfast drink of the Apollo

astronauts, with Constant Comment.
As Dad and ailing boy gazed long into the mug of
swirling Day-Glo orange weather,
each scried his special American fate and glimpsed his
future bright or dim turning
in the churning muddle and thought of saying so, but
fearful of what might at last

come true, said nothing. Then ailing boy ran off to
puke and Dad poured out the last
of the potion and both forgot the cloudy signs that
Tim McVeigh decoded in a series
of Post-Its found on 50 lb. bags of Scott's Turf
Builder years later. Remember turning
on the tube in time to see the concrete dust, cinder,
and bone blown up high enough
over stunned and screaming mothers to become a
new meaner sort of crazy weather
we've been having in these parts, an ashier nastier
warning, the spitefullest comment,

black and urgent, falling from shadowed skies over
Oklahoma City, hooded comment
grimly pointing a sooty finger east-north-east at
Manhattan's metropolis, first and last
of dream cities from which we woke to sounds of no
one grumbling about the weather?
The sky that morning—not yet. When then? Dunno,
and cried. The awfullest TV series
—don't dare say The Golden Girls! Now you just go
ahead and pick one horribilis enough
to curdle lemonade. Imagine it airing on all channels
all hours and no way of taming

to another station to watch, say, Dancing with the
Stars. Left to choose between turning
off the set or learning to love the taste of our own

throw up, how can we even comment
as the cheered lies unfurl? It's a grand old flag, anger,
waves of blame. Sure. But enough
happier pursuits or sweet liberty to fill a pilgrim's
stocking? Better hope this ain't our last
chance to run the ninnies and their nesting cries out
of town, for while the World Series
of Dullness is only now beginning, how many innings
of this blather can we weather?

From the looks of those slate-bottomed clouds, I'd
say the weather will soon be turning,
letting loose a rainy series of clichés, none of them
even rising to the doorsill of comment.
We may survive. After all, when was the last time
anything we loved lasted long enough?

INVENTORY OF PROPERTIES: ROSE THEATRE, 1598

The Lord Admiral's Men performed, among other plays, *Dr. Faustus, Tamburlaine, The Spanish Tragedy,* and *The Jew of Malta.* At times, Edward Alleyn's company shared the Rose's stage with Shakespeare's company, the Lord Chamberlain's Men

A rock, an iron cage, the mouth of hell.
A tomb for Dido, a tomb for Guido, a bedstead.
Two steeples & a chime of bells, an Esquimau.
A heifer for the play of Phaeton, her dead limbs.
A globe & scepter, three clubs, a union of great price.
Two hatchets: one of leather, one of wood. A spade.
A porpentine, two rackets for tennis, a bay tree.
Two cakes of finest marzipan. The city of Rome.
Seven lances. A pair of stairs for Phaeton.
A wooden canopy. Old Mahomet's head.

A lion's skin, a bear's skin, Phaeton's ruined chariot.
A curtle-axe, Kent's wooden leg. One skull, quite chopfallen.
Iris' rainbow, a little altar, three wall-newts, a haggard, some rue.
Neptune's fork, his garland. Sea-foam, nymphs, Triton's horn.
Eight vizards, Tamburlaine's sword and buckler, a mattock of wood.
A suit or golden armor, a sign for Mother Red Cap, phials for poison.
Cupid's bow & quiver. The cloth of the sun and moon.

Cerebus' three heads. Drake's drum & a tempest.

A fane of feathers, a tree with golden apples, an asp.
Six iron targets, one of copper, five of wood. Ten
rapiers.
Two mossy banks, the golden fleece, Helen's tortoise
combs.
Mercury's wings, Don Tasso's picture, a dragon-
helmet, a bowl of elm.
A shield with three lions, a gilt spear, Spanish figs, fog,
pig's blood.
Two piles each of Shoreditch velvet carnadine, satin,
silk & taffeta.

A pair of coffins. A bull's head. Sundry prodigies.
Three timbrels, a dragon for Faustus, a brazen head.
Hautboys, sackbuts, an ostrich, a great horse (with
legs).
A pope's mitre, tennis balls, the belly of a whale.
Green grapes. Machinery for the Siege of London.
Machinery for the beheading of Black Joan.
A crown for a ghost, a crown with a sun.
Three crowns imperial, a coronet.
A black dog. Five swart devils.
A cauldron for the Jew.

DISCOURAGING WORDS

My ears twitched in disbelief that words
so unkind could issue from the mouth of one
dressed all in gingham, of one so short of leg
and face, so small her hands and the pale curls
sun-pasted to her fragrant brow. The scent
of wild flowers hung about her always.
You compared her to cool waters and I knew
why you'd sit more lightly in the saddle
on days you saw her, and why for days after
remember how I loved cubed sugar, apples.

But then she went and said the words she said,
the words that still rankle, the words I'd done
nothing to deserve, though said as if I had.
Soon after we cleared off her patch for good,
you left me for a chance at faro.
I shied at the shot warning me you'd lost.
Next day, they cinched a strange saddle to my back
and, riderless, led me up Boot Hill behind
a pine box uneasy in the wagon bed.

To whom could it have mattered: her watching
them put you in the ground. With a big man
at each arm to keep her from falling,
she looked even smaller, her curls still paler,
as she pressed your boots to her breast and wept.
Strange how she who once had choice words enough
for both of us, had left not even one
for either you or the horse you rode in on.

DO NOT PASS GO

You ever see her riding that old B&O line?
She was the little tin shoe. I was a tin shoe too.
Sell my house on Baltic just to be on that line.

She was the little tin shoe. I was a tin shoe too.
Things got rough when the fake money got tight.
You ever see her riding that old B&O line?

Things got rough when the fake money got tight.
One day she's sipping gin from the little top hat.
Sell my house on Baltic just to be on that line.

One day she's sipping gin from the little top hat.
Next day she's vanished with what's left of the bank.
You ever see her riding that old B&O line?

Next day she's vanished with what's left of the bank.
One day after that, it's me who's headed for jail.
Sell my house on Baltic just to be on that line.

"Do not pass go," Judge says, "Go directly to jail.
Collect no two hundred dollars. Get straight to jail."
"Judge," I says, "that two hundred dollars was bail."

You ever see her riding that old B&O line?
Sell my house on Baltic just to be on that line.
Sell my little green house on Baltic to be on that line.
Cash in all my hotels just to be with her on that line.

CANANDAIGA

for Bob Atwan

The poplar shaking in the empty field
is the Tower of Babel.
The willow bending over the canal
is the time Noah drank too much.
The white balloon tied to the "For Sale" sign
is Lot's wife turned to salt.
And the forlorn paper lantern
is the fatted calf.
The planet shedding orange light
is the Book of Job.
The robed virgin atop the column
is the gift of tongues.
And all revelation
is a rough sack of dried olives
and an earthen pitcher of wine
turned to vinegar and must.

But this lake and these clouds in that sky
await their glosses in vain. And vain it is
for us to wait here beside this lake
beneath these clouds under that sky
for signs less worldly, pairings more voluptuary
which else might have figured redemption
as surely as if the type of world we live in
were not the only world in which we live.

ALSO BY JACK ROBERTS

A Life Less Damnable
Eclogues (forthcoming)